D0056174

NATOMAS USD
2500 NEW MARKET DRIVE
SACRAMENTO, CA 95835

Serving Your Country

The Thunderbirds:

The U.S. Air Force Aerial Demonstration Squadron

by Ellen Hopkins

CAPSTONE
HIGH-INTEREST
BOOKS

an imprint of Capstone Press
Mankato, Minnesota

Capstone High-Interest Books are published by Capstone Press
151 Good Counsel Drive, P.O. Box 669, Mankato, Minnesota 56002
http://www.capstone-press.com

Copyright © 2001 Capstone Press. All rights reserved.
No part of this book may be reproduced without written permission from the
publisher. The publisher takes no responsibility for the use of any of the materials
or methods described in this book, nor for the products thereof.
Printed in the United States of America.

Library of Congress Cataloging-in-Publication Data
Hopkins, Ellen.
    The Thunderbirds: the U.S. Air Force Aerial Demonstration Squadron/by Ellen
Hopkins.
        p. cm.—(Serving your country)
        Includes bibliographical references (p. 45) and index.
        ISBN 0-7368-0776-4
        1. United States. Air Force. Thunderbirds—Juvenile literature. 2. Stunt
flying—Juvenile literature. [1. United States. Air Force. Thunderbirds. 2. Stunt
flying. 3. Aeronautics, Military.] I. Title. II. Series.
UG633 .H627 2001
797.5'4'0973—dc21   00-009827

Summary: Describes the U.S. Air Force Thunderbirds, their history, mission,
aircraft, maneuvers, and team members.

Editorial Credits
Blake Hoena, editor; Lois Wallentine, product planning editor; Timothy Halldin,
    cover designer; Linda Clavel, illustrator and production designer; Katy Kudela,
    photo researcher

Photo Credits
Defense Visual Information Center, 10, 13, 16, 19
Galyn C. Hammond, 30
Kevin Vandivier/The Viesti Collection, Inc., 43
Photo Network\David Vinyard, 7; Cynthia Salter, 23; M. Bednar, 25
Unicorn Stock Photos/Jay Foreman, 39
U.S. Air Force Thunderbirds/SSgt. Kevin J. Gruenwald, cover, 8, 20, 27, 40;
    SSgt. Justin D. Pyle, 4, 28, 34, 37

1 2 3 4 5 6 06 05 04 03 02 01

**Capstone Press would like to thank the U.S. Air Force Thunderbirds for their
help and support.**

Table of Contents

Chapter 1
The Thunderbirds

The Thunderbirds' narrator tells the air show's audience to look behind them. The Thunderbird pilots are flying their F-16 Fighting Falcons into view. F-16 jet airplanes are some of the U.S. military's most advanced aircraft.

The Thunderbirds' commander signals the other pilots to hit their afterburners. These devices increase the fuel that jet engines burn. Extra fuel creates more power and increases speed. The Thunderbirds' F-16s reach speeds of up to 600 miles (960 kilometers) per hour as they fly over the audience. In seconds, they are out of the crowd's sight.

The Thunderbirds fly F-16 Fighting Falcons.

The Thunderbirds then reappear flying in a Delta formation. This formation looks like a wedge. The two aircraft on the wedge's back corners turn away. One pilot turns right. The other pilot turns left. The rest of the pilots then form a Diamond formation with their aircraft. They roll their airplanes over as they perform a loop in the air. This maneuver is called the Delta Blueout Cloverloop Opener.

Air Shows

All types of people attend air shows. Many of them share an interest in aviation. They enjoy seeing historic aircraft at air shows. They also are interested in seeing experimental aircraft. These test planes may help decide how future aircraft are designed.

People also attend air shows to see stunt flying. They watch pilots perform dangerous and exciting maneuvers with their aircraft. The U.S. Air Force Thunderbirds perform such feats.

The Thunderbirds often fly formation maneuvers. Their maneuvers display the skill

6

The Delta formation looks like a wedge.

and training U.S. Air Force pilots need. It is difficult for pilots to control their airplanes when flying close together. They need to have excellent eyesight and steady hands. They also need to trust and have confidence in the skills of the pilots flying with them.

The Thunderbirds' Mission
The Thunderbirds' mission is to build people's trust in the U.S. Air Force. Their demonstrations

The Thunderbirds have performed all over the world.

show the Air Force's combat readiness. The Thunderbirds also help recruit new Air Force members. The Air Force needs around 30,000 new members each year. Air Force officials hope that people who watch the Thunderbirds may become interested in joining the military.

The Thunderbirds also spend many hours as "Ambassadors in Blue." They represent the Air Force in many ways that do not include flying.

They visit hospitals and schools to talk about the Air Force and the Thunderbirds. They do interviews and give speeches. They answer fan mail. They even give reporters backseat rides in their airplanes.

On The Road

The Thunderbird team travels more than 200 days a year. They fly between shows that sometimes are thousands of miles or kilometers away. Between March and November, the Thunderbirds perform at more than 60 air shows. Each demonstration lasts about one hour.

The Thunderbirds have performed all over the world. They have performed in all 50 states and in more than 60 foreign countries. More than 300 million people around the world have enjoyed their performances.

Chapter 2
Thunderbirds' History

In June 1950, North Korea invaded South Korea. This action started the Korean War (1950–1953). China and the Soviet Union supported North Korea. The United States decided to support South Korea. Jet fighters were first used in air battles during the Korean War. These aircraft played a key role in this conflict.

At first, China provided North Korea with an advantage over South Korea. China had a well-equipped air force. It used MiG-15 aircraft built by the Soviet Union. These aircraft were

During the Korean War, the U.S. military began using F-86 Sabre jet fighters.

considered the best jet fighters in the world at the time.

The U.S. military wanted to produce an aircraft comparable to the MiG-15. The military then had the F-86 Sabre built. Large-scale air battles soon followed. The F-86 Sabre performed well. By the war's end, the U.S. military had lost only 58 F-86s. China had lost 800 MiGs.

3600th Air Demonstration Unit

In 1953, the Korean War ended. But the Air Force still needed pilots. Few people were enlisting in the Air Force. Most people thought only extremely skilled pilots could fly jet fighters.

Air Force leaders wanted to create public interest in jet fighters and the Air Force. They wanted to show people that almost anyone could be trained to fly jet airplanes. Air Force leaders then decided to create the 3600th Air Demonstration Unit. They stationed this unit at Luke Air Force Base (AFB) in Arizona. Many of the pilots chosen for the 3600th Air Demonstration Unit had flown in either World War II (1939–1945) or the Korean War.

The Thunderbirds first used F-84G Thunderjets.

The new unit needed aircraft. Air Force officials chose the F-84G Thunderjet. This aircraft had been used as both a fighter and a bomber during the Korean War. Its straight-wing design made it stable and easy to handle.

The 3600th Air Demonstration Unit also needed a name. During the first weeks, 3600th members called themselves the Stardusters. But later, Lieutenant General Robert Harper changed the team's name to the Thunderbirds.

The Thunderbird is a creature from American Indian folklore. American Indians believed this legendary bird of prey created lighting by blinking its eyes. The flap of its wings created thunder. Some American Indians also believed that the Thunderbird could grant victory in battles. Air Force officials thought that this bird was a good symbol to represent their demonstration team.

The First Years
The Thunderbirds first performed June 8, 1953. They flew at Luke AFB in Arizona during the flight school graduation ceremony.

The public first saw the team perform on July 21. This demonstration was at the Frontier Days' Air Show in Cheyenne, Wyoming.

The Thunderbirds performed 50 more shows in 1953. Nearly 2 million people saw them and their F-84Gs in action.

In 1956, the Thunderbird team moved to Nellis AFB in Nevada. They also began to use F-100 Super Sabres during air shows. These new jet aircraft could reach the speed

Thunderbird Patch

Captain Bob McCormick designed the Thunderbird patch. He was one of the original Thunderbird team members. Few changes have been made to the patch since its original design.

The four planes in the middle of the patch are flying in a Diamond formation. This is the Thunderbirds' basic formation.

The red, white, and blue colors of the patch represent the United States. These colors also are popular with many American Indian tribes.

The Thunderbirds began using F-100 Super Sabres in 1956.

of sound. Sound travels at about 760 miles (1,220 kilometers) per hour. The Thunderbirds used F-100s for the next 13 years.

Performances Overseas

In 1959, the Thunderbirds toured Asia. They had a difficult schedule during these demonstrations. They flew 24,000 miles (38,600 kilometers) between Japan, Taiwan, South Korea, and the Philippines. They performed 29 times in 31 days. They once finished a show and then had to fly 1,200 miles (1,900 kilometers) to the next show without landing. They arrived only five seconds late.

During their Asian tour, the Thunderbirds won the MacKay Trophy. The U.S. Air Force gives this award to pilots or groups for an outstanding achievement in aviation. It is one of the Air Force's highest awards.

Over the next decade, the Thunderbirds continued to perform overseas. They visited Europe, Africa, and the Caribbean.

The Thunderbirds' Popularity

The Thunderbirds' popularity continued to grow. On June 4, 1969, the Thunderbirds began to use the F-4E Phantom aircraft. The American Broadcasting Company (ABC) televised the Thunderbirds' first air show using these jet fighters. Nearly 10 million viewers saw the performance.

The Thunderbirds also appeared on other television shows. These shows included *The Ed Sullivan Show*, *Today Show*, and *The Merv*

Griffin Show. The pilots even appeared in an episode of *The Six Million Dollar Man*.

T-38 Talon

F-4s are fast airplanes. But they use a large amount of gas. In 1973, the Organization of the Petroleum Exporting Countries (OPEC) cut the world's oil supply. This action caused gas prices to rise. The Thunderbirds decided they needed to use a more fuel-efficient aircraft. They chose the T-38 Talon. One F-4E uses the same amount of fuel as five T-38s.

The Air Force uses T-38s as supersonic trainers. Aircraft that can fly faster than the speed of sound are called supersonic. Pilots learn advanced fighting techniques while flying T-38s.

T-38s became the only non-combat aircraft used by the Thunderbird team. They also could not be refueled in midair. The Thunderbirds then could not fly overseas to perform while they used T-38s.

The Thunderbirds had several accidents with T-38s. In one year, five Thunderbird pilots

The U.S. Air Force uses T-38s to teach pilots advanced fighting techniques.

died. The worst accident was the Diamond Crash. On January 18, 1982, four pilots were flying in a line and practicing loops. During formation flying, Thunderbird pilots closely follow their commander's lead. On that day, the commander's controls failed. His airplane then crashed into the ground. The other three pilots also crashed as they followed their commander.

Chapter 3
Aircraft and Maneuvers

Part of the Thunderbirds' mission is to display U.S. air power. They also display the Air Force's most advanced aircraft. In 1983, the Thunderbirds began using the F-16 Fighting Falcon. This jet fighter was the U.S. military's newest jet fighter. The F-16 can reach speeds of 1,500 miles (2,400 kilometers) per hour. It also can locate and bomb targets that pilots cannot see.

The F-16 Fighting Falcon is one of the U.S. military's most advanced aircraft.

Fighting Falcon

The U.S. military has used several different models of the F-16. The military began using the F-16A in January 1979. This model had a single seat. The F-16B was developed later. It had two seats. During training, student pilots sat in the front seat. Their instructors sat behind them.

In 1992, the Thunderbirds began using the F-16C and F-16D. The F-16C has one seat. The F-16D has two seats. These updated versions of the F-16 had the newest radar and avionics systems. Radar uses radio waves to help pilots locate distant objects. Avionics allows aircraft to be easily upgraded with new technology.

Today, all active Air Force units use F-16Cs and F-16Ds. The military has more than 400 F-16s in active service. In addition, the Air National Guard uses more than 300 F-16s. Reserve units have another 60 F-16s.

The Thunderbirds' F-16s are modified. These changes include a smoke system that

The Thunderbird symbol is painted on the bottom of the Thunderbirds' aircraft.

replaces the combat cannon. The smoke system trails smoke behind the airplanes. Smoke allows audiences to better see the Thunderbirds as they perform maneuvers. Another modification is the paint job. Thunderbird F-16s are painted red, white, and blue. The bottoms of their airplanes are covered with the Thunderbird symbol.

With these changes, the Thunderbirds' aircraft cannot be used in combat. But the

Thunderbird team can make them combat ready within 72 hours.

Speed
Formation flying can be dangerous. Thunderbird pilots perform most maneuvers at about 450 miles (720 kilometers) per hour.

Formation flying at such speeds leaves little room for mistakes. Only 18 to 36 inches (46 to 91 centimeters) separate the airplanes during some maneuvers. Pilots must have confidence in each other's skills when flying this close.

Solo Maneuvers
Thunderbird pilots perform several types of maneuvers. A single pilot performs solo maneuvers. These maneuvers include steep climbs, Four-Point Rolls, and Wing Walks.

Pilots performing Four-Point Rolls begin with their airplane in an upright position. They rotate their airplane so that the right wing points down. They then flip their airplane upside down.

Two pilots perform duets.

They continue to rotate their airplane so that their left wing points down. Finally, they end the maneuver by moving their airplane back to the upright position.

A Wing Walk is similar to a Four-Point Roll. But pilots do not flip their airplane upside down during this maneuver. Instead, they move their airplane from an upright position to right wing down. They then move their airplane upright again before pointing the left wing down.

Two solo pilots perform duets. The Cross Over Break is one such maneuver. The pilots start by flying in the same direction. They then turn and speed toward each other. As they approach each other, the pilots flip their airplanes sideways.

Formation Maneuvers

Formation maneuvers are among the most exciting maneuvers that the Thunderbirds perform. Several pilots fly together for these maneuvers. Formation maneuvers include the Delta Blueout Cloverloop Opener and the High Bomb Burst.

The High Bomb Burst is the team's most famous maneuver. Five pilots perform the High Bomb Burst. Four pilots fly in a Diamond formation. The fifth pilot follows behind them. They begin with a steep climb. The fifth pilot continues to climb. But the other four pilots

The Thunderbirds perform many maneuvers while flying in formation.

break from the Diamond formation. They perform loops in the air in different directions and then dive toward each other. They cross paths and loop around again. They then fly back into the Diamond formation.

Chapter 4
The Thunderbird Team

Few U.S. Air Force members are able to become Thunderbird pilots. Pilots need great skill and dedication to earn a position on the team. But Thunderbird pilots do not claim to be the best at what they do. Instead, they say that their skills reflect the talent that all Air Force pilots have. Their mission is to demonstrate this talent to others.

Women are allowed to serve with the Thunderbirds. They perform many supporting duties such as aircraft maintenance. But a woman has not yet flown for the team. Before

Few pilots earn a position with the Thunderbirds.

The Thunderbird team includes eight pilots.

1993, congressional law did not allow women to fly combat aircraft. It also takes years for pilots to become eligible to fly with the Thunderbirds. Only three female Air Force members have earned enough flight hours to fly jet fighters. In the future, there may be female Thunderbird pilots.

Officers

The Thunderbird team includes 12 officers. Eight of these officers are experienced fighter pilots. The other four officers perform supporting duties for the Thunderbird team.

Supporting officers include a flight surgeon, an executive officer, a maintenance officer, and a public affairs officer. The flight surgeon provides medical care for the Thunderbird team. The executive officer manages the team's budget, training, and personnel selection. The maintenance officer is responsible for the repair and maintenance of the team's aircraft. The public affairs officer presents information about the Thunderbirds to the public.

The most well-known Thunderbirds are the eight pilots. Six of the Thunderbird pilots fly air show maneuvers. They spend time talking to people before and after air shows. They sign autographs. They also pose for pictures in their red flight suits, white frams, and blue caps. A fram is a neck piece worn like a collar.

The remaining two pilots perform other duties. The operations officer serves as a safety observer and flight evaluator. This pilot makes sure that no other airplanes are flying near when the Thunderbirds perform. He also judges how well the pilots perform during demonstrations.

Thunderbird Pilots

Thunderbird #1	Commander
Thunderbird #2	Left wing
Thunderbird #3	Right wing
Thunderbird #4	Slot
Thunderbird #5	Lead solo
Thunderbird #6	Opposing solo
Thunderbird #7	Operations officer
Thunderbird #8	Advance pilot/narrator

The advance pilot/narrator describes the demonstrations. This officer tells the audience about the Thunderbirds and the maneuvers that pilots perform.

Pilots

To be a Thunderbird, Air Force pilots must hold the rank of captain or higher. They must have fewer than 12 years of service in the Air Force. They also need to have flown at least 1,000 flying hours and be a qualified fighter pilot.

Pilots serve two years on the Thunderbird team. The pilots' terms are split so that half the pilots are replaced each year. In this way, there always are experienced pilots on the team to help train new pilots.

Every year, Air Force pilots apply to join the Thunderbirds. The Thunderbirds' commander selects the candidates based on their skills. These pilots are then judged by the rest of the team members.

Next, the remaining pilots are tested in an F-16D. They are tested on formation flying and basic fighter maneuvers. The Thunderbirds' commander then scores their performance.

Thunderbird pilots continually practice flying.

The commander also rates these pilots on their communication skills. The Thunderbirds spend much of their time talking to people. The commander then recommends certain pilots to the Air Combat Command commander for approval.

Practice
The pilots practice from November through March. Each pilot flies more than 100 practice missions before the performing season begins.

They practice over Indian Springs Air Force Auxiliary Field. This field is located northwest of Las Vegas, Nevada.

New pilots learn the maneuvers flying solo. The Thunderbirds do not fly as a unit until the new pilots have mastered each maneuver.

At first, the pilots keep their formations loose and they fly at high altitudes. They form tighter formations and fly closer to the ground as they gain experience with the maneuvers. During demonstrations, pilots fly their aircraft within 3 feet (.9 meters) of each other.

Behind the Scenes

Currently, four civilians and more than 100 enlisted Air Force members serve in support roles for the Thunderbirds. Civilians are not members of the U.S. military. Their duties with the Thunderbirds may include scheduling air shows, helping maintain aircraft, or assisting the commander and executive officer. Enlisted members volunteer to serve on the Thunderbird team. They follow the guidance of officers as they perform their duties.

Enlisted members of the Air Force serve with the Thunderbirds for three to four years. New members go through three weeks of training. They meet the team and learn how each member contributes to the Thunderbirds' mission. They learn the team's history and its daily operations. New members then are tested on their knowledge. They must score at least 80 percent on this test to earn a Thunderbird patch.

Most Thunderbird team members are aircraft maintainers called crew chiefs. Two crew chiefs check each F-16 before and after every flight. Crew chiefs' duties include refueling, inspecting, and repairing the Thunderbird aircraft.

Some of the F-16s' systems require special training. The Thunderbird team has many specialists to work on the team's aircraft. Avionics specialists are skilled electricians. They maintain electronic wiring in F-16s. They also maintain the cabin pressure, oxygen, and air conditioning systems.

Fuel specialists oversee the emergency fuel system. This system provides power to F-16s if their main power system fails. Pilots then can land their aircraft safely. This system requires

Many specialists are needed to maintain F-16s.

a special fuel called hydrazine. This dangerous substance needs careful handling.

Many other specialists help to maintain the Thunderbirds' aircraft. Supply specialists order parts and tools. Structural specialists maintain the F-16s' frames and paint jobs. More than 30 other enlisted Air Force members handle office duties, budgets, publicity, and communications. Each person plays an important role in fulfilling the Thunderbirds' mission.

Safety

After each season, Air Force officials select 22 maintainers. During the following year, these crew chiefs travel to air shows. This group is called the "showline." Their duty is to prepare the Thunderbirds' aircraft for air shows.

Safety is important. Each Thunderbird F-16 has two crew chiefs assigned to it. They make sure the airplanes are safe for every performance. The team has never cancelled a performance due to mechanical problems.

The operations officer handles pilot and crowd safety. This officer controls the airspace for 5 miles (8 kilometers) in every direction around an air show. He will stop the show if another aircraft enters that airspace.

Life support specialists maintain the F-16s' life support system. This system includes pilots' helmets, masks, parachutes, and harnesses. Harnesses are similar to seat belts. They hold pilots in their seat as they fly.

Egress technicians maintain F-16s' canopies and ejection seats. Canopies cover airplanes'

The "showline" crew prepares the Thunderbirds' F-16s for air shows.

cockpits. Pilots escape damaged aircraft using ejection seats. In emergencies, pilots pull a handle to set off an explosive charge that blows off their airplane's canopy. Explosives in the ejection seat then send it into the air. Ejection seats hold parachutes. The parachutes open when the pilots are safely away from the airplanes. These strong, lightweight pieces of fabric allow pilots to land safely on the ground or in water.

Chapter 5
The Future

After the Diamond Crash, people began to wonder if the Thunderbird team was needed. Many people thought the pilots on this team were just showing off. These people thought the Thunderbird program was too dangerous and expensive. They also thought that these pilots had more important duties to perform.

Saving the Thunderbirds
In 1982, the U.S. House of Representatives and Senate debated over continuing support for the Thunderbirds. Representative Dan Daniels argued that it would be a great loss if the Thunderbirds no longer performed. The

In the early 1980s, people debated the need for the Thunderbirds.

Thunderbirds allow people to see military aircraft in action. They also allow people to see the skills of military pilots. Members of the Senate and House of Representatives agreed with Daniels. They issued a statement supporting the Thunderbirds.

Thunderbird fans also showed their support. During 1983, about 16 million people in 33 states watched the Thunderbirds perform. This attendance was a record for one year.

Thunderbirds' Mission

The Thunderbirds still have a mission to complete. The Air Force needs around 30,000 new recruits each year. The Thunderbirds will continue to interest people in the Air Force.

The Thunderbirds also display the U.S. Air Force's combat readiness. They will continue to display the skills needed to fly some of the military's most advanced aircraft.

The Thunderbirds continue to demonstrate the U.S. military's most advanced aircraft.

Words to Know

afterburner (AF-tur-bur-nur)—the part of a jet engine that burns extra fuel to create more power

ambassador (am-BASS-uh-dur)—a representative of a group or country

aviation (ay-vee-AY-shuhn)—the science of building and flying aircraft

canopy (KAN-uh-pee)—the cover over an airplane's cockpit

enlist (en-LIST)—to join the military

maneuver (muh-NOO-ver)—a planned and controlled movement; pilots perform a series of maneuvers during air shows.

narrator (na-RATE-or)—a person who tells a story or describes an event

parachute (PA-ruh-shoot)—a piece of strong, lightweight fabric used to drop people safely from aircraft

supersonic (soo-pur-SON-ik)—faster than the speed of sound

To Learn More

Green, Michael. *The United States Air Force.* Serving Your Country. Mankato, Minn.: Capstone High-Interest Books, 1998

Sweetman, Bill. *Supersonic Fighters: The F-16 Fighting Falcons.* War Planes. Mankato, Minn.: Capstone High-Interest Books, 2001.

Van Steenwyk, Elizabeth. *Air Shows: From Barnstormers to Blue Angels.* A First Book. New York: Franklin Watts, 1998.

Useful Addresses

International Council of Air Shows
751 Miller Drive SE
Suite F-4
Leesburg, VA 20175

**The Professional Airshow Performers and
    Producers Association (PAPPA)**
P.O. Box 8458
Norfolk, VA 23503-0458

U.S. Air Force Thunderbirds
Office of Public Affairs
4445 Tyndall Avenue
Nellis AFB, NV 89191

Internet Sites

Air Force Link
http://www.af.mil

International Council of Air Shows
http://www.airshows.org

**The Professional Airshow Performers and
    Producers Association (PAPPA)**
http://208.234.20.120/pappa/index.htm

The U.S. Air Force Thunderbirds
http://www.airforce.com/thunderbirds

Index